What We Leave Behind

MATTHEW SHEELEY

Ancient Religion

First printing: Earth Day, April 22, 2024

WHAT WE LEAVE BEHIND

What have I to say? What will be my contribution to the tapestry of existence? What will be recorded, etched forever on the canvas of time and marked with my name? How long is "forever?" Is anyone still listening? How much does any of this matter? I hope that you, like me, do not one day find yourself guilty of the crime of thinking too much instead of feeling...

It is this defining faith that runs through me: the faith that lifetimes after my own will be better off for the work I have done here. That humanity will endure and step up and surprise me. That this good, green earth may be allowed to regain some of its former glory. That the people will give that "mighty shout for life" when the time comes. This is my greatest and deepest hope.

Am I false to think myself important? Maybe so. But what choice do I have? Wiser and better men than I have trifled with it, expelled it, regurgitated it, sent it off and accepted it back, in time. Let me keep on writing until I come upon something worth saying. Let us move past motive and belief; let us get on through the slog of doubt as fast as we are able.

Soothing stillness - to my ears, a sweet symphony.
In the morning where I thrive,
still enveloped in the subconscious.
Hollow echo across the lake
and I feel its magnitude in my bones.
That I could stay...
that life could take place in this one, fragile moment...

I walk barefoot through his majesty
and God knows me well.
We acknowledge each others' presence
and go about our own affairs, uninterrupted.
I see many things and I take them each in turn:

I see the loons returning home proudly
and I love them.
I see the hawks caught high in the day
and I love them.
I see the woodpecker improvising his rhythm
and I love him.
I see the world of which I am a part
and I love it.
I love it as I love myself, for it is my Self
and my one true identity.

Praise to you, O grassy reed-
Your form is slender and fine
and your hue of verdant virility.
For many hours could I gaze
into your countless brilliant striations
wondering what kind of patience
could procure such minute perfection.
Not for the first time,
I marvel at the scale of life,
how something so small
can be so complex and organized.
It is in sheer contrast to the might
and grandeur of a mountain.
How spectacular then, to achieve
both the seamless exactness of the micro
and the staggering vastness of the global.

On occasion I enjoy indulging in the simple act
of observing the goings-on around me:
noticing, sensing, feeling and consuming...
the tiny wren chooses this moment
to explode in a cacophony of joy...
the solitary loon unleashes
its eerily beautiful melody across the lake...
a honey bee buzzes busily around my head...
See how life flourishes!
See how it maintains itself in perfect harmony;
the resonant hum can be heard in the earth.
The soil itself speaks and talks of the record
which time plays endlessly.

I come to you now to be fully endowed
with the pleasantries that you once brought.
How splendid you were
and how splendid you will be again!
For the shaken trees and the fallen leaves
and the rattling of distant forgiveness is nearby,
you have only to claim it.
I can and do stay for hours, for lifetimes.
Several pass me by and I witness them all
in the recesses of my mind.
Time does not exist; the man-made construct
and its attempt to dictate holds no bearing here.
The wind picks up when it is time
and the leaves on the trees trill in crescendo.
As soon as it has begun, it has settled back down.
Even the slightest sound may be heard,
like a teasing look into that specific time and place,
a time stamp on the world's aural history.

I cannot describe your beauty to any who ask,
I can only point to their lungs and say,
"See? See how the rise and fall comes
without pause, without thought?
See how delicate and perfect a unity
between the living and the giving?
See the elegant mastery of it all
and the starving that breeds desire?
It is also so with me
and with every living thing around us."

For life necessitates life, feeds it,
and without this companionship nothing would grow.

To all the birds in the world-
I see you and I love you.
How simple and free
your lives must be.
Primitive, primal, pointed, and plain;
I long to have purpose such as yours.
To awaken every morning
with just the one goal in mind:
survive
and live on
through the beauty of time.
The pleasure is mine
to watch you soar through the sky,
dipping and diving
like the very paintbrush of God.
You are the intersection of grace and chaos,
the epitome of joy,
and you remind me each day
of my own place in the world.

Listen carefully..
underneath it all, in the undercurrent,
you may hear the hum of the Earth-
it is the self-perfusing stream of life,
the life-blood of an ancient being.
Always it is present,
even amidst the clamor
of this modern world.
This is the singular strand
that ties all of existence-
an infinite Oneness.
To tug gently is to pull
at the literal fabric of the Earth.

Of the dance of the trees I know much.
Of the scent on the breeze,
Of the sonic trapeze,
Of this pleasant disease I also know much.
Of time-flying widowers searching for peace;
Of glad-fingered instruments, wild and free;
Of pigeonholed lovers filled up with grief;
Of toxic and terrible sweet little feet;
Of tragedy, rhythm, and man-made machines;
Of looking-glass friends and the others they keep;
Of wandering strangers with no place to be;
Of the flags in the sky I can never unsee;
Of myself and of course of the warnings I heed;
       Of these I know much, but I've hardly begun.

Of all of the history that you might need;
Of how all this matters, of what I foresee;
Of happier lives that won't disagree;
Of motherly souls who head now to sleep;
Of pleasant and plentiful powerful scenes;
Of far distant brothers who no longer weep;
Of that which we learn, which we will not repeat;
Of rapid dissention, however brief;
Of proof-ridden fables upon the marquee;
Of how they all got it who needed release;
Of these I know also, and I know them as well.
And I know now the mountain of sin.
And I know now where to begin.

Busy and counted is the world around me.
Everything moves always and to its own end.
I am not a part of it;
rather, it is told to me as if from the pages of a book,
described in rough, short details.

Or perhaps it is a painting, brushed together intently
and only hinting at its meaning
through inspired combinations.
But now it seems to come to me in a tune,
a tune layered and woven and put aside for a while.
A tune unintended to be a tune at all,
accidentally purposeful.
A tune that leads your ear so far
it forgets what it's listening for.
It has all the usual swells and harmonies
built in and executed perfectly.
It is flawless and self-sustaining.
It happens *for* me, not *to* me.

I am here to observe and report.
I am the mute sentry, guarding the rights to my mind.
I am the bearded sage, cold and cooing to the wind.

"I am" and "I exist" and all these are true.
And "the cure for the insanity of man" is true too.
Let go your petty squabbles,
your incoherent worries.
Tell me not of time worth managing
or tasks to be done.
Be here and be present;
see this world for what it is-
a gift, a haven,
to be appreciated and lived in.
An example of delicate mastery,
of relation and imperfection,
of balance and of temperance.
A wild, simple refuge
with no more meaning than is given.
Ground within your senses
and see that it is so...

Make of this body, this soul,
an antennae unto the Earth.
I am but a conduit, receiving and relaying pure Truth.
I will spend my days absorbing it openly
and allowing it to speak through me.
These are not my words I write but those of the Earth.
Through them may I distill and extract
the essence of being.
I am not special-I have simply opened my Self
and tapped into the Source.
Now may be seen clearly
the great tragedies of the world,
the mourning and the yearning of an ancient being.
If only through these pages may you know
the splendor and squalor of what is to come:
I am writing either of the magnificent downfall
of a species or its storied resurgence, I know not which.

Rhythmic savior I confess to have known,
to you I direct my attention now.
It is good and right to move and to grow;
not distasteful is the flavor of the world
but to those found in it.
Languishing long and lightly libated,
perfectly strong I come to you now
and set down gently in your arms.
Handsomely greeted, my mind takes it's seat
as the light show begins:
Currents and hazes,
brights flicker twice then extinguish,
tricks and trembles and twitches,
so sudden and exotic - I wish them well.
I see it all as it passes,
the floating phantom of my dreams.
Stay long, never leave, I beg.

I want to get lost
so I learn to cherish
safety and security.

I wish to feel cold
because only after being truly chilled
can you fully appreciate warmth.

I desire to be hungry
because food tastes better
when it is savored.

I long to be troubled
so I know what it means
to be at peace.

Let me experience deep sadness
so I may treasure pure joy
when it comes.

Teach me to thirst,
that I might drink
with intention.

Allow me my boredom
so the awesome is
more spectacular.

Take all that I have
and I will understand
wealth.

Do away with my wants
and what I truly need
shall surface.

In the journey of life,
I'd much rather have
a compass than a map.

Jealous bugs and tiny feet,
ancient tunes that swerve then meet,
delicate answers to questions we lack...
not for wanting, but stalling
those succulent hopes
we would trade for a hat.
There is not knowing, or staying,
or changing, or stopping
this flash-flooded library creek
or of healing the words
that through all ages speak
or of consummating our worth.
Fast-forward some to the edge of the globe,
when our beauty is strained and how?
Nobody knows.

There is something in the way the waves flow-
never any clear beginning or end.
A repetitive, trance-like motion
recurring for as long as you care to observe it.
It has always moved in this way
and will continue moving this way
ceaselessly, until the end of time.
Does Time have an end?
One day we shall know.
There is something in the way the waves flow

What are we here for?
And why?
What are we trying to save?
Are we trying?
We drive through you
we pass by on our way
from one place to another.
We live *beside* you, not *in* you,
you are something to be endured.
When we enjoy you,
we do it at a distance
with an oversaturated filter.
We do not experience you.
We do not get lost in you.
We run you down
for our own pleasures and desires
with no regard for the warnings you give.
We destroy you.
We massacre you.
We take more than we need.
We take more than we want.
We take
and you give
and you give
and we die
and you die.
What are we here for?
And why?
What are we trying to save?
Are we trying?

Teach me something about your world.
Is it green?
My world was green.
My world was vibrant
and lush
and a feast for the senses.
My world held patterns
and grew stubbornly
and spread itself high.
My world was green.

Teach me something about your world.
Is it alive?
My world was alive
and humming
and teeming with life.
My world breathed and smiled
and bended and swayed.
My world was alive.

Teach me something about your world.
Is it beautiful?
My world was beautiful.
My world was flawless
and breathtaking
with voluptuous curves.
My world radiated
and enticed
and brilliantly gleamed.
My world was beautiful.

Teach me something about your world.
Is it brutal?
My world was brutal.
My world was harsh
and swift
and unforgiving at times.
My world killed
and ate
and took no remorse.
My world was brutal.

Teach me something about your world.
Is it generous?
My world was generous.
My world was plentiful
and lavish
and brimming with treasures.
My world gave away
and gave away itself
until it was gone.
My world was generous.

Teach me something about your world.
Is it green?
My world was green.

I take you with me wherever I go,
be it among the silent company of the pines
or high upon the oldest parts of the earth.
I carry you along the sputtering seaside
and we float commiserate together
down each lazy river bend.
I pack you in and unfold you,
exposing you to the open air
for which you first existed.
I hold you close and layer myself in your words,
speaking them to the breeze
and waiting patiently for their return.
I am you and you were me,
only now I can't remember how...
I have found a way to speak through the ages
so that I may exist long after I have gone.
I remember writing every word.
I remember turning every phrase
til it came out the way it ought.
I remember it all.
I remember it now.

Write upon my grave:
"He did not like parades
or saying goodbye."

Touch upon your lips
a glass of brown liquor.

Share amongst the trees
a good and pleasant time.

Hold against your skin
some green and leafy thing.

Sing into the wind
a sad, reflective tune.

Press onto this page
"These arms were meant to hold."

Speak to all who ask
these words, so I might live.

And thus far I have said all I can think to say, all I know to be true. For most it will seem to be nothing of note - the vague ramblings of a delirious fool, to be sure! - but to those who seek more, who find themselves outnumbered in this box-office world, I hope you take something like wisdom from me. I'll leave what I've learned; take it, if it helps!

Pick it up. Carry it for a while. When you feel moved, take it out and unfold it to the open air. Expose it to the world and allow it to change, if it must. When it is time, pack it away and carry it on. Reflect on it often and you will find that it has changed - or have you? Come the end of your days, you must pass it on; simply leave it for someone else to find. And so I will live on through time and so you.

Dig in the dirt, touch an ageless tree, sit in a quiet green place. Listen to the hum of the Earth - it is still there, how-ever faint, despite our own attempts to drown it out. Be still and present - *be* rather than be *doing*. And so the Earth will not endure, but flourish! What we leave behind: this is what we have to say; this is how we will be known.

Now we come to it -
will we leave anything behind at all?

WHAT WE LEAVE BEHIND